An orchestration of feelings

Nishka Kakulapati

BookLeaf Publishing

India | USA | UK

Presentation by *BookLeaf Publishing*

Web: www.bookleafpub.com

E-mail: info@bookleafpub.com

ISBN: 9789363304789

First edition 2024

*To my Aunt Deepthi for putting her faith in me
and my writing , I'm forever grateful .*

ACKNOWLEDGEMENT

I want to thank my mum and my dad who had to listen to me read my poems to them and gave me the best advice that i could have asked for to push through and create a version of my work that i am proud of ,I love you both . And to all of my family and friends for constantly supporting me and my dreams , this would not be possible without any of your support and love. Thank you.

Picture perfect

Our mind is an unedited movie
Filled with the most brutal thoughts
And the strongest of emotions
It's true contents are known to no-one but the
owner

The words that are spoken and the persona that
is portrayed
Is a sham that is filtered to the liking of each
individual
Words are lies.
Emotions are practised.

Everything you see is a picture perfect movie
Edited for the gain of one and to prevent the loss
of another...
You see what they want you to see
Not what is truly real

The world is a movie
And everyone in it is playing a carefully
manicured part.

Lights, camera, action and begin...

Liquid Sunshine

Peacefully running around carefree,
While dancing in the droplets of liquid sunshine
They trickle down her face, sending a cold
shiver down her spine
She glides gracefully as the veil of her dress
Flows perfectly,
Her locks of curls bouncing tirelessly,
In the middle of the nights adversity.

When I look into the mirror

When I look into the mirror
my reflection is what I see
but is my reflection
someone I want to be?
I see a person
who is full of hatred and jealousy.
Hiding behind a layer of insecurities
I bring myself closer so that I can see my face
I notice something other than perfection
My eyes are suddenly filled with rage.
Why can I see the gaps in between?
When it took me so long to cover up what was
Left of me..
All that masking was a waste
If I'm still not satisfied with
What I see in the mirror
 Everyday

Villains Version

When we read fairy tales
we're told the end comes when the hero saves
the day,
They get their happy ending
while the villain is made to pay

Have you ever wondered ?
If the villain was the hero before their wicked
ways
Perhaps instead of getting an idyllic ending
they ended up with a great load of pain

No one is born an evil doer,
they are all just people who are too afraid
To allow themselves to love
So instead they mask on a callous face

Happiness

5

The feeling you get when the sun caresses your
face
or when you're laying down making angels in
the snow
The glimmer in your eyes when you get to
witness someone you love, grow

The sound of birds harmonizing in unison
or the beauty of an enchanting conversation
The proud feeling of fulfilling a great , ambition

The throbbing pain in your stomach when your
attacked with laughter
or the smile in your eyes
when you realise you're someone who's opinion
is sought , after

The day we met

I walk into a cafe
Craving some caffeine
For the long road trip ahead of me
I go to the barista who is waiting patiently.
Awaiting my order as the whole place is empty.
I frantically search the vast menu for what I need
The whole time her eyes are glued to me
Still unsure I utter pleasantly;
" A cappuccino and a ham sandwich please"
She smiles as I pay then walks away
To make her first order of the day

As she works , I search for a seat
Where the rays of the sun can shine onto me
Tiredly, I lay my head on my hands
Staring out the window, towards barren land
Before I can drift of to sleep
Dreading the hours of driving ahead of me
The Barista comes over to me and says ;
"Your order is ready sir , don't go to bed"

Before she leaves , I quickly go
"I love your shirt , that quotes from my favourite
show "
Her face lights up with a joyful glow

She responds " No way its my favourite too'
Then she proceeds to sit down
And our conversation continues
With an unending flow
Neither of us wanting to, let go

Mood

Like the ripples of water that flow along the sea
bed
That suddenly grow into engulfing waves
My mood changes,
Depending on the incidents of the day.

Sadness overpowered by a tide of laughter
Or happiness that changes motion
Into temper
The gust of air that changes the current,
From low to high.
An indecipherable drift of emotion that happens
inside.

The little voice Inside my head

An eager whisper lingers waiting to be heard
Words mumble as they slip of my tongue
Praying I don't say what's inside my head.
Because that voice is deadly
So unfiltered and transparent
That it's cruel and unforgiving
Ready to sink anyone to the ground
And watch smiling as it goes under
But that is me.
It's not the version of me that anyone knows or
hears,
It's the person who comes out when nobody sees
The only one who knows my true identity
It may only be a whisper but it started a scream.
And I don't know how much longer I can live,
Without setting it free

Late night drives

The moons glistening in the spotlight
As the specks of glitter sparkle throughout the
twilight sky
My heads rested against the car door
At peace like the pleasant luminescent
Azure , which borders all life
A tune playing in my ears
As the many cars travel by
My body engulfed in the harmony
Of the symphony of my late night drives

Motherhood

Motherhood, is being selfless
Motherhood, is giving everything without
expecting anything back
Motherhood, is tolerating anger directed to you
Motherhood, is the strong willed feeling of
always wanting to keep your child safe
Motherhood, is being supportive
Motherhood, is never failing to show up
Motherhood, is knowing your childs needs and
feelings at all times
Motherhood, is being a stable rock even when
the ground is shaking
Motherhood, is loving without bounds
Motherhood, is valuing your mother
As without her , the world would cease to exist

Soul ties

The people who are my family away from home
The ones who have watched me mature
And grow
The people who share my agony , hardships and
grief
The ones with whom I create everlasting
memories with whenever we meet

The people who consistently have my back
The ones who make sure I'm on the right track
The people who prove to be my ride or dies
The ones with whom I share eternal soul ties

Fictional Fantasy

My imagination drifts me to my own literary
paradise
As the dormant words written on a page
Are active in my thoughts,
And are brought to life in my mind,
I curate my own perception of what I believe the
characters are like

From the colour of their hair
To the type of clothes they wear
From the emotions that they feel
To believing they're real.

Their battles aren't fought alone
Their struggles reflect my own
A different world readily available
From the comfort of home.

Invisible string

We have met before.
Although my memory can not support.
We passed each other in the middle of a
populous street.
By accident, assuming it would be the last time
we would "meet"
5 years later , we crossed paths again
This time not as strangers but as friends.
Later the friendship bloomed into something
more
Into a companionship with the person,
who is now the one I most adore.

Growing pains

I don't want to grow up.
I don't want my life as I know it now , to become
a distant memory
I don't want my "golden years" to fade away
I don't want everything around me to be
unfamiliar and change.
But..
I want to grow up so *I* can evolve and change
Into someone who is still me , just at a different
age
To understand the world even more,
All its pleasures and pains
Life's hurdles and uncertainties
After Breaking out of my teenage cage.

Concept of the mind

The concept of the mind
is like a leaf on a tree
stuck together like the thoughts in your brain
but lingering to fly away like the words you
wish to say
Your thoughts don't have a pause button
 they are constantly on play
ready to unmask the biggest idea of the day!
Your mind is your greatest possession
let it live up to the potential it generates
and don't ever allow people to dictate
what ideas your mind creates...

F.A.M.I.L.Y

17

Follow you through the stages of life
Act as a shoulder to lean on
Making memories together through,
Interwined experiences
Lend you a listening ear for your grievances
Yearn to keep up their appearances

Beauty of silence

We live in a noisy world
Where we are surrounded by sounds,
Imagine we could make everything quiet
And just take a look around

The loud will become quiet
The unnoticeable will be seen
Instead of your ears working,
Your eyes will show you the scene

Survival of the fittest

Humans are wired to always want to be the best
of their kind
The richest, the most popular , the one envied
among the ton
A constant state of competition,
Among everyone

You strive to be the lion and fear being the
wildebeest
Either a leader who orders
Or a subject forced to follow
A king of the jungle , high on a pedestal
Or just another body being pushed in the crowd.

The need to be superior
Outways human morality
The greediness of power
Strips you of your complaisant personality
Your heart shrinks as your ego grows
Until increasing status is the only thing you
know

A desire to be the one most alive

And to be the one who continues living a
faultless life,
A race that turns man against man
Leaving you the most paralysed inside
All because of the time bomb ticking inside that
says...

Survive.Survive.Survive.